4/14

EXPLORING COUNTRIES

Poland

by Walter Simmons

BLASTOFF! READERS
5

BELLWETHER MEDIA • MINNEAPOLIS, MN

Note to Librarians, Teachers, and Parents:

Blastoff! Readers are carefully developed by literacy experts and combine standards-based content with developmentally appropriate text.

Level 1 provides the most support through repetition of high-frequency words, light text, predictable sentence patterns, and strong visual support.

Level 2 offers early readers a bit more challenge through varied simple sentences, increased text load, and less repetition of high-frequency words.

Level 3 advances early-fluent readers toward fluency through increased text and concept load, less reliance on visuals, longer sentences, and more literary language.

Level 4 builds reading stamina by providing more text per page, increased use of punctuation, greater variation in sentence patterns, and increasingly challenging vocabulary.

Level 5 encourages children to move from "learning to read" to "reading to learn" by providing even more text, varied writing styles, and less familiar topics.

Whichever book is right for your reader, Blastoff! Readers are the perfect books to build confidence and encourage a love of reading that will last a lifetime!

This edition first published in 2012 by Bellwether Media, Inc.

No part of this publication may be reproduced in whole or in part without written permission of the publisher. For information regarding permission, write to Bellwether Media, Inc., Attention: Permissions Department, 5357 Penn Avenue South, Minneapolis, MN 55419.

Library of Congress Cataloging-in-Publication Data
Simmons, Walter (Walter G.)
 Poland / by Walter Simmons.
   p. cm. – (Blastoff! readers–exploring countries)
 Includes bibliographical references and index.
 Summary: "Developed by literacy experts for students in grades three through seven, this book introduces young readers to the geography and culture of Poland"–Provided by publisher.
 ISBN 978-1-60014-732-6 (hardcover : alk. paper)
 1. Poland–Juvenile literature. I. Title.
 DK4147.S56 2012
 943.8–dc23   2011033447

Printed in the United States of America, North Mankato, MN.

010112   1203

Contents

Lithuania

Gulf
of
Gdańsk

Baltic
Sea

Kaliningrad,
Russia

Did you know?

The modern symbol of Warsaw is a mermaid holding a sword and shield. According to legend, a mermaid helped to build the city of Warsaw and still protects it.

Warsaw ★

Poland

Germany

N
W   E
S

Czech Republic

Slovakia

Belarus

Ukraine

Poland is a country in central Europe that covers 120,728 square miles (312,685 square kilometers). To the west of Poland is Germany, and to the south the Czech Republic and Slovakia. Poland's eastern neighbors are Ukraine and Belarus. Warsaw, the capital of Poland, sits in the eastern part of the country.

Lithuania and Poland share a short border in the northeast. Kaliningrad, a **province** of Russia, also borders Poland in the north. The Baltic Sea meets Poland's northern seacoast. The **ports** of Gdańsk and Gdynia lie on the **Gulf** of Gdańsk, an **inlet** of the Baltic Sea.

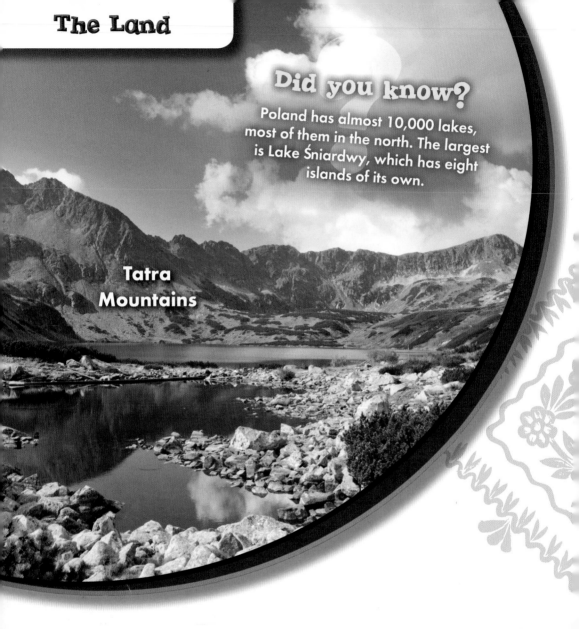

Did you know?

Poland has almost 10,000 lakes, most of them in the north. The largest is Lake Śniardwy, which has eight islands of its own.

Tatra Mountains

Poland is a mostly flat country. Its landscape begins with lowlands in the north and gradually rises into mountains along the southern border. The Tatra Mountains cross the border into Slovakia. This range includes Rysy, which reaches 8,199 feet (2,499 meters). This is Poland's highest point.

Poland's longest river is the Vistula. This river begins in the Carpathian Mountains, then winds east and north and passes through Warsaw. The Vistula empties into the Baltic Sea at Gdańsk. The Oder River also flows north and forms part of the border with Germany.

fun fact

The Baltic seacoast of Poland is one of the world's major sources of amber. This is ancient tree resin that turns hard as rock over thousands of years. Some ancient amber pieces contain insects that are now extinct.

Baltic Sea

The Bialowieza Forest

Today much of Poland is farmland. However, a dense forest once covered its plains. The forest disappeared wherever people settled and cleared the land. The Bialowieza Forest is what is left of this once large forest.

Bialowieza lies along the border with Belarus. It includes huge oak trees, some of them more than 500 years old. Long ago, the Bialowieza Forest was a hunting range for the rulers of Poland and Russia. It also served as a safe hiding place for people in wartime.

hoopoe

The forests of Poland offer natural **habitats** for wild animals, including foxes and lynx. The Bialowieza Forest shelters wild boars, deer, wolves, and wisent. These European bison feed on grasses and leaves. They are the biggest land mammals in Europe. Mountain goats, wolves, and the European brown bear roam the mountains. The plains of Poland are also home to a small number of wild horses.

wisent

corncrake

European eel

fun fact

The Baltic Sea is home to flounder, cod, salmon, and the European eel. This long fish looks like a snake with fins.

Storks, eagles, and herons nest in trees along the Baltic seacoast. Cranes, snipes, and corncrakes live in meadows. The forest is home to orioles, nightingales, and the hoopoe. This bird has a long bill and a crown of orange feathers.

Did you know?
In 1978, John Paul II became pope, or leader of the Roman Catholic Church. He was the first pope to come from Poland.

Poland has a population of more than 38 million people. Most have Polish **ancestors**, and the majority are **Catholic**. They speak Polish, which is the country's official language. Before **World War II**, Poland had the world's largest Jewish population.

Some Germans, Ukrainians, and Belarusians live in Poland today. Small numbers of Roma still remain in Poland, too. The Roma are a people group that came to Europe from India hundreds of years ago.

Speak Polish!

English	Polish	How to say it
hello	cześć	CHESH-ch
good-bye	do widzenia	doe vee-ZEN-ya
yes	tak	tahk
no	nie	ne-YEH
please	prosze	PROH-shuh
thank you	dziękuję	jen-KOO-yuh
friend	kolego	koh-LAY-go

In cities, Poles live in small apartments and use **trams** and buses to get around. A subway line runs north and south through the city of Warsaw. Many Poles use it to get to work in the morning. Few families have cars, but most people own bicycles.

Trains link the cities to small towns. In **rural** areas, people live in simple homes. Farmers rise early and use tractors and horse-drawn carts to tend their fields. Many families raise cows for milk and meat, and chickens for eggs.

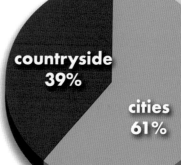

Where People Live in Poland

countryside 39%

cities 61%

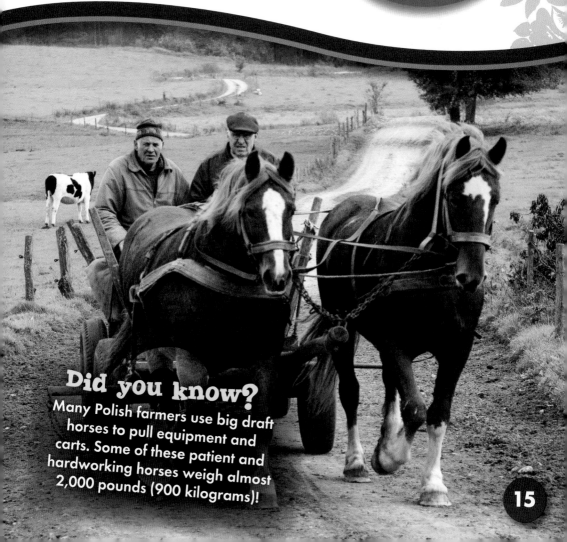

Did you know?
Many Polish farmers use big draft horses to pull equipment and carts. Some of these patient and hardworking horses weigh almost 2,000 pounds (900 kilograms)!

In Poland, school starts with preschool at age 5 or 6. Elementary school lasts six years. Students study math, Polish, technology, art, music, and physical education. A three-year **gymnasium** follows primary school. Gymnasium courses include foreign languages, religion, and **civics**.

Students then continue to secondary school. They may attend a **vocational school** or a *lyceum*. A *lyceum* prepares students for advanced studies in medicine, law, engineering, and other fields. In their last year, *lyceum* students take the *matura*. If they pass this series of difficult exams, they can go on to a university. It takes at least three and a half years to get a university degree in Poland.

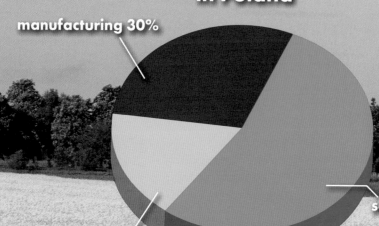

Where People Work in Poland

manufacturing 30%

services 53%

farming 17%

! **fun fact**

Polish workers dig salt out of deep underground caves. Salt mining has been a tradition in the city of Wieliczka for around 900 years.

More than half of all Polish workers have **service jobs**. They work for banks, grocery stores, and post offices. Polish factory workers make cars, steel, clothing, food products, and machinery. Shipbuilding is a major source of jobs in Poland. Gdańsk, on the Baltic Sea, is one of the largest shipbuilding ports in the world.

In southern Poland, many Poles work in coal mines, steel mills, and chemical factories. Polish farms produce grains, potatoes, apples, and livestock. Most family farms are too small to support an entire family. Farmers often take on additional work in nearby mines or factories.

handball

Soccer is the most popular team sport in Poland. Handball is another favorite. In this sport, two teams throw a ball around and try to score goals. The Poles are also strong in wrestling, weightlifting, and boxing. Many kids join sport clubs to practice their skills in soccer, tennis, swimming, and track-and-field.

In the summer, Polish families often take vacations to the Baltic seacoast. They like to try wakeboarding, water-skiing, or sailboarding. During the long winter, Poland's mountains offer skiing, ski-jumping, and the dangerous **luge**.

luge

lazanki

fun fact

Poles love a variety of sausages, which they call *kielbasa*. Different regions of the country make their *kielbasa* with different meats, spices, and herbs.

In Poland, most meals consist of **hearty** foods. Many people skip lunch and eat a big dinner in the late afternoon. This meal often begins with *barszcz*, a thick red soup made with beets. Cooks serve it hot in the winter and cold in summer.

For the main course, beef, pork, or chicken is served with potatoes, noodles, or cabbage. Fish is also popular, especially near the seacoast. *Lazanki* is a favorite noodle dish that contains cabbage, sausage, and often mushrooms. Everyone in Poland eats *pierogi*. These are small **dumplings** filled with meat or vegetables. Another popular food is *bigos*. This thick stew has cabbage, sausage, and other meats. For dessert, Poles enjoy cheesecake or *paczki*, a small cake filled with fruit.

barszcz

pierogi

Christmas and Easter are two of the most important holidays in Poland. Christmas celebrations begin on December 6, when St. Nicholas gives children gifts. On Christmas Eve, families gather for a large meal with many courses. For Easter, Poles use many different techniques to decorate eggs. On Easter Sunday, it is tradition for Poles to bring food to church so that it can be blessed.

On November 11, Poles celebrate the day in 1918 when their country became an independent nation after **World War I**. Poles fly flags, and the country's leaders give speeches. In Warsaw, runners dressed in red and white take part in an Independence Day Run. **Constitution** Day on May 3 is Poland's other major national holiday.

Easter

fun fact

The national symbol of Poland is a white eagle. It appears on buildings, coins, and even the jerseys of the Polish national soccer team.

Every hour, a trumpeter plays the Hejnał from the tallest tower of St. Mary's Basilica in Kraków. All Poles know this musical phrase by heart. Many centuries ago, Mongols from Asia invaded Poland. When they reached Kraków, they swarmed through the city. A trumpeter ran to the top of the church to play the Hejnał as a warning.

Poland has been invaded many times throughout its history. Each time, Poles have risen up and saved their country. Today, the trumpeter in the tower of St. Mary's turns in four directions while playing the Hejnał. The tune is a symbol of Polish resistance, determination, and unity.

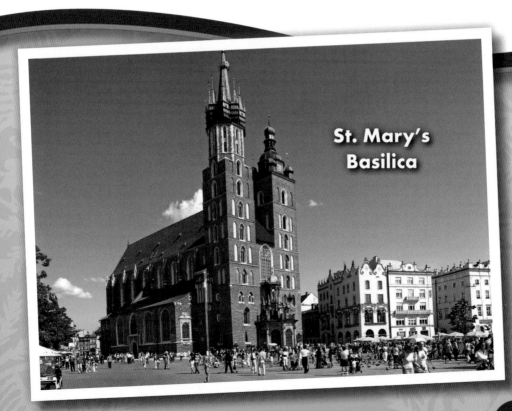

St. Mary's Basilica

Fast Facts About Poland

Poland's Flag

The Polish flag is red and white. These were the symbolic colors of Poland. Upside down, the modern flag matches the flag of Indonesia. Poland's flag was officially adopted in 1919.

Official Name: Republic of Poland

Area: 120,728 square miles (312,685 square kilometers); Poland is the 70th largest country in the world.

Capital City:	Warsaw
Important Cities:	Kraków, Łódz, Wrocław, Poznań, Gdańsk
Population:	38,441,588 (July 2011)
Official Language:	Polish
National Holiday:	Constitution Day (May 3)
Religions:	Christian (92%), Other (8%)
Major Industries:	farming, fishing, manufacturing, mining, shipbuilding
Natural Resources:	coal, lead, iron ore, sulfur, salt, silver, copper, zinc
Manufactured Products:	cars, clothing, cement, fertilizer, machinery, ships, steel, furniture
Farm Products:	grains, potatoes, cherries, plums, tomatoes, cucumbers, apples, dairy products, pork
Unit of Money:	złoty; the złoty is divided into 100 groszy.

Glossary

ancestors—relatives who lived long ago

Catholic—members of the Roman Catholic Church; Roman Catholics are Christian.

civics—the rights and duties of citizens

constitution—the basic principles and laws of a nation

dumplings—balls of dough often filled with meat or vegetables

gulf—part of an ocean or sea that extends into land

gymnasium—a three-year middle school that follows primary school in Poland

habitats—the environments in which a plant or animal usually lives

hearty—filling and comforting

inlet—a small natural bay formed where the sea meets the seacoast

luge—a sport in which a person sleds feetfirst down an ice track

ports—sea harbors where ships can dock; ships from around the world deliver and pick up goods in Poland's ports.

province—a division of a country; a province follows all the laws of the country and makes some of its own laws.

rural—characterized by farmland and the countryside

service jobs—jobs that perform tasks for people or businesses

trams—small city trains powered by electricity from overhead wires

vocational school—a school that trains students to do specific jobs

World War I—a world war that lasted from 1914 to 1918; the Allies defeated the Central Powers in World War I.

World War II—a world war that lasted from 1939 to 1945; the Allies defeated the Axis Powers in World War II.

To Learn More

AT THE LIBRARY

Brooks, Susie. *Let's Visit Poland*. New York, N.Y.: PowerKids Press, 2010.

Deckker, Zilah. *Poland*. Washington, D.C.: National Geographic, 2008.

Zuehlke, Jeffrey. *Poland in Pictures*. Minneapolis, Minn.: Twenty-First Century Books, 2006.

ON THE WEB

Learning more about Poland is as easy as 1, 2, 3.

1. Go to www.factsurfer.com.

2. Enter "Poland" into the search box.

3. Click the "Surf" button and you will see a list of related Web sites.

With factsurfer.com, finding more information is just a click away.

Index